REORGANIZING THE FEDERAL BUREAUCRACY

REORGANIZING THE FEDERAL BUREAUCRACY

THE RHETORIC AND THE REALITY

MICHAEL P. BALZANO

American Enterprise Institute for Public Policy Research
Washington, D.C.

Michael P. Balzano was the director of ACTION from 1973 to January 1977.

ISBN 0-8447-3264-8

Library of Congress Catalog Card No. 77-84326

AEI Studies 165

Printed in the United States of America

CONTENTS

ACKNOWLEDGMENTS

I would like to acknowledge all those who assisted me in the preparation of this monograph. Their criticism and their advice played a significant role in its preparation. Special thanks go to Professor Irving Kristol, Dr. Austin Ranney, Dr. Howard Penniman, Dr. Jeane Kirkpatrick, Dr. Karl Cerny, and Dr. Nelson Polsby.

I would also like to thank Ronald L. Gerevas and Frank Tobin for the roles they played throughout the reorganization and for the use of their resources in preparing this article. Special thanks go to Ms. Elizabeth Prestridge, who assisted me during the research, writing, and editing of this monograph.

1
INTRODUCTION

During the presidential campaign of 1976, candidate Jimmy Carter's pejorative references to the federal bureaucracy earned him the title "the anti-Washington candidate." His promises to reorganize the federal government were punctuated by frequent allusions to the bureaucracy as a bloated, wasteful, inefficient mess. Candidate Carter accurately read the antibureaucracy mood of most Americans and clearly conveyed the message that if elected President he would reorganize the federal government to make it more efficient. Moreover, since his electoral victory it is equally clear that the mood of the American people on this issue has intensified. In a national poll taken two months after the election, 56 percent responded that they believed the President would reduce the number of people on the federal payroll.[1] In a similar poll taken four months later, between 64 and 77 percent believed that government workers were too numerous, were overpaid, and received more benefits and did less work than non-government workers.[2]

In light of the public response to his antibureaucratic campaign rhetoric, it is little wonder that the newly elected President quickly petitioned the Congress for authority to reorganize the executive branch of government. Based on statements made by Bert Lance, the director of the Office of Management and Budget (OMB), administration officials, and the President himself, reorganization will be aimed at a number of objectives:

- the elimination of unnecessary government structures;
- an increase in the efficiency and effectiveness of government services;

---

[1] "Great Expectations," *Newsweek,* January 24, 1977, p. 20.
[2] George Gallup, "Federal Workers Held in Low Public Esteem," *Washington Post,* June 12, 1977.

1

- the elimination of duplication and overlap;
- a reduction in the volume of regulations, policies, and guidelines;
- the reassignment of decision-making responsibilities to the lowest possible levels;
- an increase in accountability;
- an improvement in the relationship between federal, state, and local governments; and
- a simplification of government so that the average citizen can understand it.[3]

In view of the attention given to the federal bureaucracy during the 1976 campaign, any reorganization aimed at these objectives would probably win the support of the majority of Americans.

Many of these objectives were pursued and, to a significant degree, reached in a series of reorganizations executed from 1973 to 1976 within ACTION, the federal agency for volunteer service.[4] In 1973, a thorough review was undertaken of the agency's programs and operations. The results of this review pointed to the need to restructure the agency in light of current program needs. That restructuring is completed, and this study is presented in the belief that a record of that experience may be useful to those now seeking to reorganize the federal bureaucracy. The same obstacles that ACTION encountered most surely will be encountered on a larger scale in President Carter's reorganization attempts. ACTION's personnel moves were influenced by Civil Service rules, regulations, and constraints that will also apply to personnel moves necessitated by the President's reorganization. Congress will scrutinize every detail of the President's plan, jealously guarding its legislative offspring, just as it did with regard to ACTION's reorganization. And, of course, civil servants can again be expected to initiate lawsuits to preserve their power, authority, and livelihood.

ACTION's turbulent history during these four years offers a case study of the problems the President may face. The following pages

---

[3] See Office of the White House Press Secretary, *President's Reorganization Authority,* April 1977; "OMB: A More Personal Style of Management," *Government Executive,* vol. 9, no. 2 (February 1977), pp. 10-11; testimony of Bert Lance, director, Office of Management and Budget, in U.S. Congress, House of Representatives, *Providing Reorganization Authority to the President,* hearings before a subcommittee of the Committee on Government Operations, 95th Cong., 1st sess., on H.R. 3131, H.R. 3407, and H.R. 3442, March 1, 1977; testimony of Bert Lance, director, Office of Management and Budget, in U.S. Congress, Senate, *To Renew the Reorganization Authority,* hearings before the Committee on Government Operations, 95th Cong., 1st sess., on S. 626, February 8, 1977.

[4] For a comprehensive discussion of the results of these reorganizations, see "ACTION: 'How Government Should Operate,'" *Government Executive,* vol. 8, no. 8 (August 1976), pp. 36-40.

present that case and its possible ramifications. In Chapter 2, we examine ACTION and its reorganizations from 1973 through 1976. In Chapter 3, we examine the reorganizational parameters President Carter has established, and, using the ACTION experience, we identify problems the President may face in reorganizing on a grand scale.

2
ACTION: A CASE STUDY IN REORGANIZATION

By any objective standard, ACTION is a small federal agency. It has an annual operating budget of about $190 million—compared with $130 billion for the Department of Health, Education, and Welfare (HEW)—and a work force of only about 1,700 employees. Its origins can be traced to the creation of the Peace Corps in 1961, marking the federal government's first effort in voluntarism. Peace Corps volunteers make a commitment to work full time for two years in the developing world, organizing self-help projects for the poor. In 1964, the Congress created VISTA (Volunteers in Service to America) under the Office of Economic Opportunity, as a "domestic Peace Corps." Like Peace Corps volunteers, VISTA volunteers serve full-time, organizing assistance for those in need, and are paid a subsistence living allowance.

Shortly after the creation of VISTA, the Foster Grandparents Program went into operation in the Office of Economic Opportunity. Foster Grandparents are low-income senior citizens who work part-time in institutions for children with special needs, predominantly in homes for the mentally retarded. They are given a small income supplement for their services. The Retired Senior Volunteer Program (RSVP), launched in 1971 in HEW, is designed to give senior citizens of all income levels an opportunity to perform part-time community volunteer work. These volunteers serve without remuneration, usually for only a few hours a week.

The Organization of ACTION

On July 1, 1971, by executive order, President Nixon consolidated these and other programs into one independent volunteer agency, ACTION. The domestic programs were removed from their parent

5

agencies and were placed, with the Peace Corps, under the leadership of a single director, who reported to the President. In early 1973, I became the director of that agency.

The agency is divided into two basic units: International Operations and Domestic Operations. International Operations is responsible for all aspects of programming the some 6,000 Peace Corps volunteers—identifying suitable work projects and obtaining agreements with host country officials—as well as for arranging for their travel overseas, training them, taking care of their day-to-day needs, and a host of other administrative duties. Most of the International Operations staff is located in sixty-two developing nations. The Washington headquarters support staff is organized into three regional units: Latin America; Africa; and North Africa, Near East, Asia, and Pacific.

Domestic Operations, in addition to its core headquarters staff, has employees in ten regional offices, and in 1975 it had three to five employees in each of its forty-seven state offices. The Domestic Operations staff is responsible for programming for 4,200 VISTA volunteers annually, training them and providing administrative support. In addition, it makes grants to community sponsors for the administration of some 180 Foster Grandparents projects (15,000 volunteers) and 680 RSVP projects (220,000 volunteers), as well as several other programs. Recently, Domestic Operations was given the additional responsibility of recruiting, screening, and placing thousands of Peace Corps and VISTA volunteers annually.

The Need for Reorganization

Reorganization presupposes a perceived need. ACTION's reorganization grew from a perception of three basic problems that diminished the effectiveness of its operations. The first concerned the failure of ACTION's full-time volunteer programs to adapt to a changing environment. The second concerned centralized bureaucratic control. And the third regarded the lack of administrative and programmatic integration after the merger of all of ACTION's component programs into one agency.

The Changing Environment. VISTA and the Peace Corps, ACTION's two full-time volunteer programs, were created in the early 1960s. Both their programmatic thrust and their administrative systems reflected national and international conditions of the 1960s. However, both environments had changed in the second decade of these two programs. For example, Peace Corps host countries, which had accepted

6

young, college-educated generalists in the early 1960s, wanted more mature volunteers with more practical skills in the 1970s. Originally, Peace Corps recruiting and programming were designed to meet the needs of emerging third world nations, with simple infrastructures, at a low level of technological complexity. By the 1970s, a more sophisticated developing world demanded a more sophisticated Peace Corps. Agronomists, metallurgists, electrical engineers, and chemists, with advanced degrees and experience, not only were more difficult to recruit, but also required more planning and coordination with host country officials to be used effectively. In these circumstances, Peace Corps recruiting and programming systems were totally inadequate.[1] The ACTION recruiting division, a $12.2 million bureaucracy in itself, required an average of 148 days just to process a Peace Corps application.[2] The average Peace Corps volunteer began his job no less than a year after the host agency made the request. It was not unusual for a newly arrived volunteer to discover the job had been cancelled in the interim.

One of the Peace Corps' persistent problems arises from the attempt to increase the size of the program beyond its natural ability to grow. The pressure to increase the number of volunteers from Washington is transmitted all the way to the host country. Hence, to satisfy superiors, requests are made for volunteers without a firm commitment on the part of host country ministries. When the request arrives in Washington, a massive recruiting process begins in order to fill the request, whether or not the request is valid. Often, the country staff, recognizing that there is no firm program behind the request, cancels it, resulting in "request erosion." Erosion is discussed in an April 1976 memorandum by a Peace Corps research analyst:

> Counting the deductions (minuses) since the last report, you can see that in two weeks time we have had 43 requests cancelled and an astounding loss of 92 percent in predicted input. Although some of these losses were compensated for

---

[1] A programming task force analyzed the entire process from the request for a volunteer to the arrival of a trainee in the country that made the request. Country Directors were presented with the task force findings in August 1976 at a programming conference for the entire Peace Corps held in Columbia, Maryland. It was concluded that "Peace Corps does not have a programming system according to most interviewees. It does have portions of one. The Peace Corps Manual sections describe an administrative system for obtaining volunteers rather than a programming process. . . . Program quality control has virtually disappeared. There is no consistent system or practice for reviewing the quality or the content of project plans or proposals." See Willard L. Hoing, "A Review of the Peace Corps Program System," in "Proposed Peace Corps Programming System," mimeographed (Washington, D.C.: ACTION, August 15, 1976).

[2] Memorandum from Ronald E. Gerevas, director, Office of Recruitment and Communication, ACTION, to ORC (Office of Recruitment and Communication) staff, August 2, 1974, p. 1.

by other additions, the fact of these drops at such a late time in the year should give us pause. I have had a heavy flow of cancellations coming through this office recently, a good many of which are due to weak positions for requests—slots have been cancelled at the last minute (not due to "crises"), or were never really firmed up with ministries. In my opinion, much of this erosion is manageable.[3]

Unfortunately, programs are often cancelled too late in the process to stop recruiting and processing. More often than the Peace Corps likes to admit, volunteers arrive in a country long after the program has been cancelled. For example, in August 1975, 186 volunteers arrived in one African country when only 130 had been requested. Congressional staff investigators were told that even the 130 was an inflated request.[4]

Similar recruiting problems plagued ACTION's domestic programs. American communities that had previously accepted young volunteers recruited nationally now wanted locally recruited volunteers, who reflected the cultural profiles of their own population. This was a major philosophical departure. Communities had come to resent the intrusion of "outsiders" into their territory. They wanted local volunteers, who conformed to local mores and life styles and avoided the culture clashes and the social and political confrontations which characterized VISTA's early years. But the recruiting operation was designed for national, rather than local, recruiting, and was totally out of step with local desires. Like the dinosaur, the full-time volunteer programs were headed for extinction because of their inability to adapt. Each year the programs' disasters fulfilled the dismal prophecies, and yet the same systems were continued, only to fail again.

The Problem of Centralization. ACTION's domestic programs were conceived during a period when the philosophy of centralized decision making—that is, control from Washington—was in vogue. ACTION's Washington headquarters controlled almost every aspect of local program activity. Program design, budget, and operation all were determined in Washington. In many cases, those who had the most say about the style and substance of program activity in a given community had never seen that community. Washington's domination over program operations was apparent in the distribution of employees. In 1973 ACTION personnel were distributed as follows: in the Washington

---

[3]Memorandum from Linda Muller, Peace Corps research analyst, to John Dellenback, associate director for International Operations, April 1976.

[4]See U.S. Congress, House of Representatives, *The Peace Corps in West Africa, 1975*, Report of a Staff Survey Team to the Committee on International Relations, 94th Cong., 2nd sess., February 23, 1976, p. 12.

headquarters there were 778 employees providing services to the domestic programs; in the ten regional headquarters there were 255 employees; and attempting to administer service to 800 programs in forty-nine states were 44 employees.[5] This may be called an inverted pyramid of power: this highly centralized organization was largely unresponsive to the ever increasing demands for local participation and local control.

The Need for Administrative Integration. ACTION was created by a presidential executive order that placed a number of different government programs under one agency umbrella. Such a merger, it was reasoned, could lower the total cost of the individual programs by consolidating, into one unified system, administrative operations common to all programs. Beyond the financial advantages of economies of scale, it would be possible to integrate programs in the field. Young VISTA volunteers, for example, could work alongside senior citizen volunteers. The ACTION staff could learn from one program what might be useful to another.

In 1973, two years after the merger, few of these objectives had been realized. Program costs, which should have dropped, either held constant or were rising. Program operations that should have been consolidated continued to function independently. The same was true of the administrative divisions. The various programs were joined together in a patchwork quilt, with little regard for organizational symmetry.

ACTION's regional offices, which should have consisted of ten uniform administrative units, bore little structural or functional resemblance to one another. Each had a different chain of command; employees performing similar duties had different job classifications and salaries; and there was little similarity in the division of duties and position descriptions. One staffing analysis found there were approximately seventy-five different position descriptions for the twenty-seven positions assigned to each regional office.[6] Moreover, there were two field structures, one for recruiting and one for programming, with different personnel systems and without programmatic links to each other. In attempting to describe the organizational disarray in 1973, an ACTION management analyst wrote the following:

The historical approaches to resource allocation were the root

---

[5] U.S. Congress, House of Representatives, *Oversight Hearings on ACTION Agency,* hearings before the Subcommittee on Equal Opportunities of the Committee on Education and Labor, 94th Cong., 1st sess., April 9–10, 1975, p. 196 (hereinafter cited as *Oversight Hearings on ACTION Agency*).

[6] Ibid., p. 189.

of a considerable amount of organizational confusion. Funds were allocated to regions on the basis of regions' promises to spend, with continual cutting and pasting from headquarters to make it come out even. . . . The result of delegating staffing level analysis to the regions was that staff size developed disproportionately to workload, there was a pattern of increasing the staff positions in the regional offices at the expense of line positions in the field, it was much easier to work around problem employees than to improve or eliminate them, jobs took on unrelated responsibilities to support higher grades or to accommodate "special" circumstances, responsibilities overlapped and chains of command diffused, jobs were not comparable, and headquarters was left with no objective basis for evaluating or prioritizing regional requests.[7]

The Goals of Reorganization. In order to bring administrative systems into harmony with the programs, in order to bring programs into harmony with programming needs and conditions, and in order to bring the loosely connected administrative entities under a more comprehensive structure, the entire agency had to be reorganized. This was accomplished by a series of reorganizations, directed toward the following objectives:

- decentralization of program design, program approval authority, and budget authority from Washington to the state and regional offices;
- consolidation of all overlapping or duplicated functions;
- elimination of obsolete or inessential functions, transferring manpower to the state offices;
- harmonization of all program and administrative functions with current domestic and international needs; and
- reduction of administrative and program costs.

Carrying Out the Reorganization

Shortly after becoming the director of ACTION, I took a series of steps to provide ACTION employees with a clear picture of the direction in which I intended to lead the agency. The employees were fearful of the administration's plans for the agency, and their morale was extremely low, because many of them mistakenly believed the President in-

---

[7]Memorandum from Michael Dole, management analyst for Domestic Operations, ACTION, to Dana Rogers, executive officer for Domestic Operations, ACTION, December 30, 1975, pp. 1–2.

tended to dismantle the agency. This climate of fear was augmented by a number of factors:

- The President had delayed the appointment of a director for several months subsequent to the departure of the previous director.
- There was extensive media coverage of the administration's intention to dismantle the Office of Economic Opportunity.
- ACTION had no legislation of its own and had operated for two years under the precarious authority of an executive order.
- A few news stories covering my appointment incorrectly reported that I had been selected because I had written a doctoral dissertation hostile to the VISTA program. In fact, my thesis was supportive of VISTA but critical of its departure in recent years from its original goals.
- Because of my personal affiliation with national ethnic organizations, it was rumored that money would be taken away from other minorities and given to ethnics and that ethnics would be appointed to the exclusion of other minorities to top agency positions.

In addition to these suspicions and rumors circulating around ACTION, the staff was concerned about the new directions I had charted for the agency. Some of the groups that I was seeking to involve in agency programs were perceived, by some agency personnel, to be hostile to agency programs and to poor people in general. These groups included organized labor, private industry, and national ethnic fraternal organizations.

The ACTION Institutes. To overcome these apprehensions, and to create an understanding of the programmatic changes I envisioned for the agency, six ACTION Programming Institutes were held. The institutes were run under the auspices of the Center for Action Research of the University of Colorado. A cross-section of employees, from secretaries to presidential appointees, met in the field for one-week seminars. For the first time program officers in the field had an opportunity to exchange views and problems with people from headquarters who for years had been just names on paper or voices on the phone.

Most importantly, the institutes focused on educating Washington personnel to the need for sharing program design and operation with local community residents. Labor, religious, ethnic, and civic leaders participated in frank and open exchanges with large gatherings of ACTION staff. These local leaders shocked many Washington employees with their resentment at being excluded from government programs. These leaders charged the antipoverty program with denying their groups assistance on the grounds that they neither wanted nor were eligible to participate. Local civic leaders told of their resentment against Washington decision making which rode roughshod over local values, mores, and elected leaders.

The institutes represented an attempt to answer whatever questions ACTION employees had about their future and the future of the agency. They were told the goals drawn up for the agency did not depart from the original objectives of the founders of the programs or the congressional sponsors of the agency, and that they would participate fully in any reorganizations.

Finally, though we never promised that employees would not be transferred, demoted, or dismissed, we did promise that all those who worked hard would be rewarded by career advancement and promotions.

In keeping with the promises made at the ACTION institutes, not one new structure was put into place without the establishment of task forces including representatives of the affected employees. Thus, extensive employee participation, weeks of analysis, and months of testing occurred before a final plan was adopted. Participation on such task forces required sacrifices by the employees: in order not to disrupt the flow of essential services to our program recipients, new systems had to be constructed while the old ones continued to function.

Problems in Reorganization

By and large, employees at ACTION were truly excited by the challenge of reshaping the agency. A sizable majority of those surveyed, anonymously, before and after participating in the ACTION institutes felt that unless ACTION changed its internal structure the agency could not survive.[8] Hundreds of employees emerged from the institutes ready to assist in every way. At the same time, many problems surfaced. The first reorganizations, though they had been supported by the employees, clearly demonstrated that such exercises had a dollar and cents impact on their lives.

Decentralization. Our first reorganization had as its objective shifting power, not people, from Washington to the field. Better and faster service to program recipients required decision making to be transferred to the lowest level possible. The transfer of program, budget,

---

[8]University of Colorado, Center for Action Research (CAR), "ACTION Institutes, Summary of the Report, July 1973–January 1974," CAR Document No. 43 (Boulder, Colo.: University of Colorado, CAR, 1974), p. 285.

and general administrative authority from Washington or regional headquarters to the state and local levels had a significant impact on ACTION employees. As some employees gained decision-making authority, others lost it, presenting our first problem. Federal pay scales are based upon several factors beyond experience, education, and seniority. The number of employees one supervises and the level of decision-making authority are factors that establish grade and, therefore, salary. As we transferred the power to control decisions to the field, the classification ratings of those employees who lost authority dropped. In accordance with Civil Service regulations, those who held these positions had to be "downgraded" to a level commensurate with reduced authority.

After employees have been downgraded, they are given special consideration by the Civil Service Commission. They are placed on a repromotion eligibility list and must be considered for all job openings at their former grade level. If they rank among the top five candidates competing for a position, they are automatically selected for it, regardless of the qualifications of the other candidates. At ACTION, in order to repair morale, the reinstatement of downgraded employees was given a top priority. As a result, in many cases marginally qualified employees were given positions that would have gone to others in the work force. This policy, however, merely transferred the problem of low morale to the qualified candidates who were not selected.

The second major difficulty occurred when it became necessary to transfer duty stations from one city to another. Our objectives could not be met without the decentralization of some employees with their functions. Every attempt was made to assist those who did not wish to move to find another job in the same location, but, in some cases, there was no alternative except to relocate or be terminated. Our personnel office accurately predicted that, given management's objectives to relocate basic administrative services to the field, many employees would be forced to leave the agency rather than accept a transfer. This, we learned, was especially the case with ACTION employees married to other federal employees. A shift of duty station for either spouse triggered a family crisis. If the unaffected spouse could not find a federal job in the new area, one of the family members had to abandon a federal career. Given the large number of women professionals working in government, such decisions can be difficult. Should a GS-13 husband leave his $25,000 a year position, or should his GS-13 wife leave her $25,000 a year position? Even if husband and wife are not earning equal salaries, the departure of one of them from the federal payroll can plunge the family into an economic crisis. If, for example, a GS-13 husband is transferred to a rural area and his wife is a GS-7 government secretary earning $12,000 a year, it is doubtful that she will find an equivalent salary in the private sector in such an area.

ACTION had some success in transferring Washington employees to other jobs in Washington because, while ACTION was vigorously decentralizing, other Washington-based agencies were not. Had all the agencies in town been decentralizing at the same time, however, there would have been a serious number of casualties.

Employee Resistance. As the effects of the reorganizations began to be felt, employee resistance began to create serious problems. In some cases, there was apparent distortion of data by those charged with evaluating experiments. An example can be drawn from ACTION's experience in restructuring its recruiting operation. A great many congressional complaints and inquiries dealt with applicants to the Peace Corps and to VISTA. Frustrated by months and, in some cases, years of delay in receiving reports on their applications, they registered angry complaints with their representatives in Congress.

Congress was assured that the agency would increase the efficiency of applicant selection, and an intensive time and motion analysis of the entire process was conducted. This analysis, the first ever made of the recruiting division, produced a number of disquieting findings:

- It took an average of 148 days just to process a Peace Corps application, and 102 days for a VISTA application.
- For every volunteer who was ultimately accepted, an average of seven applications were processed. In the case of scarce skilled applicants, from ten to twelve applications were fully processed for every assignment.
- The recruiting process was not coordinated with the programming process. For example, 38 percent of the applications fully processed for VISTA had no links with any requests for a program.[9]

A substantial portion of our applicant processing problem stemmed from the fact that the entire procedure, including the final decision-making authority, was centralized in Washington. Our analysis proved that this recruiting operation was both unresponsive to our program needs and cost inefficient.

The system for recruiting, selecting, and placing volunteers was established in 1961. Essentially it operated as follows. All requests from host governments were held in Washington, and thousands of applica-

---

[9] Though a comparable figure was never computed for Peace Corps, it was estimated to be more than double this figure.

tions were also held in an "applicant pool," also in Washington. From time to time, placement officers would match an applicant with a particular request. This system had numerous shortcomings:

- Recruiting was not tied to programming. Hence, applicants could not choose an assignment; they simply applied to serve.
- The process took so long that a large portion of applicants with other options did not wait for notification of acceptance or rejection.
- Once an application was in the pool, information concerning its status was almost impossible to obtain.
- The vast number of employees exercising control over the applications not only increased the time and cost of processing, but also made assignment of responsibility for quality control impossible.

In order to develop a better system, a number of experiments were conducted, aimed at four basic goals: (1) to develop a system that tied recruiting to specific programs; (2) to reduce the number of days needed to process a Peace Corps application (by this time, we had reduced it to seventy-nine days merely by fine tuning the old system, but this was still not adequate); (3) to reduce the volume of applications coming into Washington, that is, to lower the ratio of applications processed to volunteers accepted; and (4) to lower the cost of the entire operation.

One experiment, the Latin American Pre-Slot Experiment (LAPSE), tested the effect of decentralizing Peace Corps applicant processing from Washington to the field and instituting a system called pre-slotting. Pre-slot is the term for the system whereby a volunteer is recruited for a specific job in a particular country. Volunteers who agree to join the Peace Corps under this system know in advance exactly where they will be going and what task they will perform. The initial experiment testing this system (LAPSE) was conducted in the Latin America region because requests from that part of the world were for more specific skills and were, therefore, the most difficult to fill.

The experiment showed that the efficiency of the entire recruiting operation could be greatly improved: the time needed to process an application could be reduced from seventy-nine to nineteen days. Moreover, the ratio of applications processed to volunteers assigned had been 7 to 1 and fell to 1.8 to 1.[10] Still another benefit was the increase in the number of requests for volunteers that could be filled. This was particularly beneficial, since program fill-rates had been

[10]LAPSE Task Force, "Final Report, Latin America Pre-Slot Experiment (LAPSE)," mimeographed (Washington, D.C.: ACTION, November 11, 1975).

gradually declining over a five-year period. Yet, despite the positive findings, a summary attached to the final report deemed the experiment a failure: "Based on the LAPSE experience, the Task Force recommends against any further pre-slotting of Peace Corps programs using the LAPSE model."[11]

The task force was able to reach this conclusion only by ignoring the positive findings of the experiment. Management's most sought-after objectives which, in fact, were the principal reasons for testing a new system, were casually brushed aside.

> Results in the other, systems-related areas—reduced confirmation time, lower applicant to trainee ratios and cost effectiveness—were considered relatively less important by the task force.[12]

It should be noted that permanent implementation of the experimental model would have resulted in decentralization of most of the functions and the staff of the Washington processing and placement division. Hence those who conducted and evaluated the experiment faced transfer to the field offices along with their transferred functions.

Other forms of internal resistance were more subtle but no less visible. Convinced that the new recruiting process would hurt the program, several Peace Corps Latin America staff members were opposed to the pre-slot concept. They saw to it that objectives were set for the LAPSE experiment that were, by any standard, inordinate. For example, the San Francisco regional recruiters were asked by the Latin America staff to recruit, among other things, an expert on the gray whale. The recruiters were horrified and protested what they saw as a contrived request, designed to discredit the new system's ability to fill the volunteer requests. But the regional director, Donald L. Brown, decided that if an expert on the gray whale was requested, they would find one. As a result of a herculean effort by Brown and his staff, from the handful of gray whale experts in the country one was located who, when informed about the Peace Corps, decided to join. After the Latin America region learned the volunteer had been found, however, the "gray whale" program was cancelled.

In some cases, foot dragging was apparent in setting up experi-

---

[11] Ibid., pp. 1–2.

[12] Ibid., p. 1. Ultimately the pre-slot system of recruiting was adopted. The cost savings from fine tuning the old recruiting system along with the vastly improved new system lowered ACTION's total recruiting budget from $12 to $5.2 million in four years. Moreover, in December 1976 the new system produced the highest program fill rate for Peace Corps. See memorandum from John Dellenback, associate director for International Operations, ACTION, and Ronald E. Gerevas, associate director for Domestic Operations, ACTION, to all ACTION staff, December 27,1976.

mental systems: due dates were not met, and supervisors did not assign adequate manpower to the job. In other cases, relatively inexperienced and low-level employees were assigned to direct projects deemed top priority. At critical phases, employees serving on task forces left their assignments to go on vacation.[13] In one case, an entire project was temporarily derailed because the person assigned to revise a recruiting catalog prior to its distribution failed to meet a critical Friday deadline and then left for the weekend, taking along all the needed materials.[14] When the catalog was finally printed, it contained information deemed so grossly inaccurate by the Latin America staff that the regional director demanded that a new catalog be printed. One of the inaccuracies alleged to be so misleading as to warrant a new printing of the catalog was the statement that volunteers would travel to their work sites in Colombia by jet aircraft, when in fact only turbo props were available.[15] In the ensuing clash between department heads, the case was brought to the agency's deputy director for resolution. After reviewing the "inaccuracies," the deputy director, John Ganley, a veteran Washington administrator, found no justification for printing a new catalog. Declaring that "he would not pay twice for the same job," he closed the discussion and ordered the participants to carry on. Despite these orders, the Latin America staff, on its own initiative and with its own budget, produced a new catalog and sent it to the field.

Destructive Rumors. Some Washington employees travelled across the country warning recruiters and domestic field personnel that the new system being tested not only would jeopardize the jobs of their Washington comrades, but also was intended to destroy ACTION programs. The following quotation demonstrates the frustration felt by agency officials dealing with rumors designed to undermine the experiment:

> From the beginning we have experienced discouraging pessimism and insufficent positive support. Needless to say, the catalogue situation is a good example. Had LA [Latin America Region] more readily responded when the need was great, the catalogue could have been much better. Other examples include purported statements to our recruitment staff that if the pool concept is replaced by pre-slotting the Peace Corps

---

[13]This also occurred during the Peace Corps Programming Task Force proceedings in July and August 1976.

[14]See memorandum from Ronald E. Gerevas, assistant director, Office of Recruitment and Communications, ACTION, to ACTION Deputy Director John L. Ganley, September 12, 1974, attachment, pp. 1-2.

[15]Ibid., p. 1.

will "die" and the presence of a poster in LA representing the experiment as a can of worms. What is ironic is that while we received a very positive reaction from the Country Directors and the teams were very warmly welcomed overseas, the Region & IO [International Operations] headquarters remain somewhat less than ecstatic about the experiment. I can well understand their concern about fill rate, etc. but would think that they would welcome the experiment and enthusiastically support it with whatever assistance was necessary. It is, after all, in an effort to better serve the Region that we are expending all this extra effort.[16]

Memos circulated through the agency predicted that major program failures would result from ill-conceived systems. This information was passed on to the Congress, prompting congressional inquiries. A widespread rumor that the experimental recruiting systems were seriously damaging the programs brought about the following inquiry from the chairman of one of ACTION's Senate oversight subcommittees:

> I understand that recent Peace Corps recruitment statistics indicate that only 47% of the Fall recruitment goal has been met, even though the goal itself is lower than that of last year.
> I would appreciate having a full report on this situation. I am also concerned that a similar situation might exist with respect to VISTA recruitment and would thus appreciate as well your providing me with a full report on VISTA recruitment progress.[17]

We responded as follows:

> Around the first of April of 1974, someone at ACTION started a rumor that the Fall recruitment for Peace Corps was down, and that only 47% of the Fall goal had been achieved. Since it would have been impossible for anyone to prematurely predict such failure, ACTION's management referred to the incident as "the April Fool Projection."
> About the time that the Agency went through its budget hearings, officials at OMB said that they had received calls from ACTION employees warning that "Fall recruitment had *failed!*" At that, I became concerned that the practical joke had been carried too far or that it was not a practical joke, but rather someone who was bent on causing unnecessary grief for ACTION's recruitment officials.

---

[16] Ibid., p. 4.

[17] Letter from Senator Alan Cranston to ACTION Director Michael P. Balzano, November 13, 1974.

18

From the technical wording of your November 13 inquiry, it is clear that you are referring to this same rumor.[18]

We presented data showing that the new systems were in fact far superior to the old ones:

In the case of Peace Corps our Fall input is currently projected at 950 against an Office of Recruitment and Communications goal of 915 or 104% attainment. The input figures may vary slightly due to the few remaining Fall programs which have not started. For VISTA, we have put in 627 trainees for a 101% attainment against an Office of Recruitment and Communications goal of 619 volunteers.

In summary, the Fall season for both Peace Corps and VISTA appear to be in good shape.[19]

Of all the rumors to come from the agency, by far the most costly was one concerning fiscal irresponsibility—that the agency was withdrawing from Peace Corps countries because it had overspent the Peace Corps budget and was now adjusting to correct for the imbalance. The rumor was so demonstrably false that none of the senior management expressed concern when it was first heard, and several friendly Congressmen telephoned to warn that agency employees "were at it again."

Early in December 1974, just before the initiation of the major field decentralization plan, all congressional committee staff and those members who cared to listen personally were briefed on the ramifications of the plan. Suddenly the ranking Republican member of the House Subcommittee on Equal Opportunities, which had no jurisdiction over the Peace Corps, elevated the bankruptcy rumor to the White House by writing to President Ford and demanding my removal as director.[20] Even though our records clearly showed that we were operating below authorized ceilings, a simple denial of the rumor was insufficient once the President had become involved. We notified the OMB that the agency was initiating a mid-year review of the entire agency. The unprecedented mid-year review not only cleared the agency of charges of fiscal irresponsibility but also provided an oppor-

---

[18]Letter from ACTION Director Michael P. Balzano to Senator Alan Cranston, December 5, 1974.

[19]Letter from ACTION Director Michael P. Balzano to Senator Alan Cranston, December 27, 1974.

[20]Letter from Congressman William A. Steiger to President Gerald R. Ford, December 18, 1974.

tunity to discuss each of its major systems improvements.[21] Later at a White House meeting on the "problems" at ACTION, OMB assured the Domestic Council staff that the agency was fiscally sound.

Discouraging Employee Cooperation. At ACTION we found many employees eager to seek innovative ways to increase efficiency, but the fact that the next innovation could threaten their livelihood often dampened their enthusiasm. In some cases, cooperating employees braved the danger of abolishing their own jobs only to encounter resistance from other departments involved in the experiment. Division heads attempting to keep their division morale high enough to conduct valid experiments were discouraged by other divisions engaged in the same experiments.

> One last point: It has been sufficiently challenging to get my own staff enthusiastic and excited about the experiment. Needless to say, they are potentially the most threatened if it proves successful. The staff which I now have working on the experiment are highly competent and well-motivated. They are enthusiastic about some of the prospects of successfully pre-slotting for Peace Corps. On the other hand, we have not enjoyed, in my opinion, a reciprocal level of support and enthusiasm from the LA [Latin America] Region and IO [International Operations].[22]

As implied above, these employees were testing, among other things, the transfer of their own functions to the field. Eventually these "enthusiastic and excited" Washington-based employees were left without a function to perform. Their office was abolished two years later.

Problems in Regional Decentralization. Another ACTION experience showed that reorganization plans were not secure against major resistance even when the employees themselves participated in them. In one case, the employees who designed and tested a reorganization plan filed an administrative appeal against the agency for making it operational. They protested the regional decentralization, that is, the transferral of the duty stations of some employees from regional headquarters to locations closer to the programs. Although we had expected transfers out of Washington to the field to be a problem, we did not expect staff already in the field to object to transfers within the

---

[21] All departments had been ordered to prepare a report of all undertakings and accomplishments between July 1973 and December 1974. These reports were transmitted to the ACTION deputy director and submitted both to OMB and to the Domestic Council in January 1975.

[22] Ronald E. Gerevas memorandum of September 12, 1974, p. 4.

regional field structure. ACTION's ten regional offices are located in major metropolitan centers—New York, Boston, Denver, San Francisco, Dallas, Seattle, Philadelphia, Chicago, Atlanta, and Kansas City—all offering a high quality of cultural life. Many employees were reluctant to move to areas with less cultural diversity. Ironically, the employees were being transferred to the area they were already responsible for servicing. Those in charge of servicing Louisiana had been based in Dallas, those in charge of servicing St. Paul, in Chicago, and so on throughout the ten federal regions. Yet, the agency became ensnarled in legal battles and administrative proceedings before the Civil Service Commission as employees argued that the regional reorganization constituted political harassment. After an examination of the evidence, including the fact that the employees themselves had written and signed the plan, the examiner sustained the agency's authority to implement the plan.[23] The problems of centralized government arose almost as much from regional centralization as from Washington centralization.

Punishing Those Who Cooperate. Finally, we learned that those who cooperate with management to change the organizational status quo must walk a hard road. Neither the laws nor their fellow employees are kind to them. The rules of the Civil Service Commission work against those who cooperate. Many employees restructured their own departments. In some departments they decentralized many of their functions and took voluntary downgrades. Management praised these employees and pledged to reward them. Later, when openings were found for them which would have restored their grades, we learned to our horror that the Civil Service rules require all "involuntarily" downgraded employees to have preference over employees who are "voluntarily" downgraded.

The second type of punishment was even more cruel than the impersonal rules of the Civil Service Commission. This was the bitter treatment accorded to cooperating employees by fellow workers who fought to preserve the status quo. Dozens of employees were warned repeatedly that if they cooperated with management to change ACTION systems, they would never again be welcome in the company of their fellow workers. Such animosities tore apart ten-year-old friendships. Many employees gave up their career status to accept a politically appointed noncareer position, so that management could transfer them from one key spot to another. When the Ford presidency

---

[23]Transcript of hearings on appeals before the U.S. Civil Service Commission Federal Employee Appeals Authority, David R. Bigger, appeals examiner, San Francisco, California, March 14, 1975, pp. 43–46.

ended, they could not return to their career jobs and risked being terminated from their federal careers altogether.

It must be kept in mind that the great majority of employees worked with management to restructure the agency, and that many of those who resisted structural changes truly believed they were saving the programs from an uncertain fate. However, a few such well-meaning employees, occupying strategic positions, can derail major management decisions.

A serious problem is that there are few inducements for employees to cooperate. At one senior staff meeting we discussed the possibility of increasing the size of the programs in several states. Veteran managers were quick to point out that the personnel in those states would have an increased workload but no increase in pay, since the Civil Service rules do not consider workload in determining grades. In many cases, employees confound management decisions because there are no rewards for implementing them.

The Politics of Reorganization

ACTION's proposed reorganizations created tensions not only within the agency but also within the administration and between the agency and Congress.

OMB Oversight. ACTION was created to consolidate all federally sponsored volunteer efforts, but it soon became evident that many other federal agencies had statutory authority to operate volunteer programs. The ACTION Office of Policy and Planning identified some thirty different federal agencies with such authority. Occasionally this proved embarrassing, when ACTION grantees withdrew from its programs to obtain higher funding from other federal programs. OMB was requested to provide comprehensive budget data on this question, but it had neither the data nor the time and manpower to research the alleged shared authority. We provided OMB with our analysis and requested that we be allowed to assist other agencies using volunteers by sharing our program models. We received unofficial word that ACTION's attempt to "grab power and money" from other agencies would not come to pass. The idea of streamlining government programs by eliminating duplicate authority among federal agencies apparently proved too controversial for OMB to discuss in writing: we never received a response to our inquiry.

Congressional Oversight. It is the Congress which enacts the laws the President must "faithfully execute." During their tenure in the legislature, congressmen become attached to statutes they pass. Some laws even bear the name of the legislators who introduced them as bills— the Taft-Hartley Act, for example, and the Landrum-Griffin Act. In other cases, legislators who were the prime movers behind a particular government program become the resident authorities on that program. Most Americans know that the Peace Corps was created during the administration of President Kennedy, but Senator Hubert Humphrey (Democrat, Minnesota) and Congressman Thomas E. "Doc" Morgan (Democrat, Pennsylvania) spoke about a peace corps long before candidate Kennedy, and are regarded as its fathers. Neither of these men took this responsibility lightly. In key congressional committees overseeing the Peace Corps, they were able to stop or change policies that might have altered the basic operation of the program as they conceived of it.

The creation of ACTION was an attempt to streamline the federal government by grouping under one rubric a number of similar programs. Yet, senators from both parties, seeking to protect specific volunteer programs placed beneath ACTION's umbrella, agreed to the merger only on the condition that the identity of each program be preserved. That is, VISTA, Foster Grandparent, Peace Corps, and RSVP volunteers, and their supporting personnel, had to be clearly segregated. The result was to destroy any hope of eliminating duplicated functions. Thus, in 1973, two years after ACTION's creation, nearly all of ACTION's component programs continued to operate just as they had before the merger.

Proposed changes in program design, operation, or agency support mechanisms brought the awesome power of legislative oversight upon us, regardless of the economic or programmatic justification for the changes. For example, ACTION developed a management system, the Integrated Programming and Training System (IPTS), which integrated major program components. This management tool simplified program operations and decentralized power and authority to newly created state offices. IPTS reduced the number of program guidelines from 206 to 100, the number of forms from eighty-seven to eleven, and the number of program systems from six to one.[24]

We began our reorganization under the assumption that Congress would support the installation of systems that strengthened the capability of federal employees to serve program needs at the local level. Instead, the plan brought immediate congressional complaints to the Civil Service Commission:

---

[24] These statistics appear in the 1974 mid-year review and were presented to the Congress during the congressional oversight hearings in April 1975. See *Oversight Hearings on ACTION Agency*, p. 187.

I believe the proposed DO [Domestic Operations] reorganization also should not go forward at this time. The proposed DO reorganization involves the elimination of some 28 positions presently occupied in Regional Offices and proposes duty station transfers generally for the persons in these positions.[25]

In regard to several proposed reorganizations, most members of Congress supported the status quo, regardless of its cost. Few congressmen intercede on behalf of fiscal responsibility and efficient government when there are no other incentives. If they should intercede, their reward will probably be complaints, usually instigated by the employees of the affected agency. Employees can induce congressional intervention in a number of ways:

(1) As constituents of the congressmen. Congressmen are highly protective of federal district and regional offices located in their constituency. They bring high-salaried jobs for their constituents and intimate contact with the dispersal of federal money. In 1975, ACTION's management considered a plan to reduce the number of regional offices by 50 percent. The plan, which was approved by OMB and the Domestic Council, called for a reduction in two phases: from ten to seven, then from seven to five. The ACTION employees in those offices informed their congressmen about the "loss" this would represent. Warnings began streaming in from Capitol Hill; each affected congressman let ACTION know that if the price of reorganization was the diminution of the federal presence in his state, the plan would not be approved. The plan was abandoned.

(2) The march to Capitol Hill. Early in the Nixon years, groups of employees protesting changes in particular programs marched on Congress seeking policy reversals. The tactic soon caught on and became an accepted practice not only for proposed program changes, but also for reorganizations that either changed the employees' duty stations or abolished their functions.

(3) Pressure from the program's constituency. By circulating rumors of grant and program reductions, the employees can mobilize an assault upon the Congress consisting of letters, telephone calls, telegrams, and demonstrations, as well as visits from program recipients. They can have an awesome impact, and the thought of irate constituents pounding on the chamber door can trigger congressional opposition to any change in the status quo.[26]

---

[25] Letter from Senator Alan Cranston to Robert E. Hampton, chairman, U.S. Civil Service Commission, December 30, 1974, p. 3.

[26] See Evans and Novak, "Nixon's Strategy on Poverty Bill," *Washington Post,* April 19, 1974, for a discussion of lobbying tactics used in the effort to save the Office of Economic Opportunity programs in 1974.

(4) The invisible alliance between the congressional staff and agency personnel. With each election, a fresh crop of congressmen and a new team of presidentially appointed agency and department heads come to Washington and attempt to seize control of the federal mechanism. These leaders come and go, but the agency personnel and the Capitol Hill staff remain as permanent fixtures of the system. Over time, these two groups have come to depend on each other for information, advice, and help. The agency employees relieve the Capitol Hill staff of the burden of the enormous volume of constituent mail and constituent case work. A seasoned congressional staffer can call the right person in an agency and get favorable action on the grant renewal application of his boss's key constituent. The congressional staff, in return, helps the agency by persuading a congressman or senator to give it a healthy budget. When a congressman challenged a proposed reorganization, we could usually trace it to an attempt by one of his staff members to protect the job of an ally in the agency.

(5) The influence of former employees serving in key positions on the congressional staff. Former ACTION staff and volunteers working in the legislative branch had an enormous impact in preventing programmatic or structural changes in the agency. The former staff, many of them also former Peace Corps and VISTA volunteers, were quick to oppose changes that adversely affected their comrades still with the agency. Former volunteers were generally sympathetic to maintaining the status quo of the program's philosophical direction.

Charges, Allegations, and Controversy

Throughout the reorganizations the agency was the center of controversy, and what was taking place was obfuscated by a host of ancillary issues.

Legal Controversies. Just before the agency announced its first reorganization plan, the Civil Service Commission released findings of a desk audit and job classification review, after which it ordered the agency to downgrade a number of employees. These employees, who mistakenly believed that the downgrades were initiated by the agency, sought relief from the chairman of the one Senate subcommittee overseeing ACTION. Weeks of meetings between the agency and Senate staff followed. Despite official letters from the Civil Service Commission to the chairman of the subcommittee assuming full responsibility for the downgrades, the Senate staff held the agency responsible.

At the height of the controversy, the Civil Service Commission was petitioned by some of these employees, along with some U.S. senators, to stop the reorganizations on the grounds that they were illegal, in violation of the merit system, and politically inspired. Although this petition was largely addressed to alleged activities that occurred prior to my tenure as director, ACTION's reorganizations were said to be the last chapter in a continuing pattern of political discrimination. These suspicions resulted from events that occurred in 1971. Shortly after ACTION's creation, charges were made by ACTION employees that the agency's management had engaged in an attempt to violate the merit system by hiring employees from the career civil service on the basis of partisan politics. These charges were investigated in 1972 and could not be substantiated. One year later, as a result of the Civil Service Commission desk audits and subsequent downgrades, employees complained of continuing political harassment. They alleged that the original 1972 politicization was continuing, this time through employee downgradings initiated by the agency. In 1974 the Civil Service Commission informed both these employees and an inquiring senator that the agency was, in fact, under orders from the commission to effect the downgrades.[27] Despite this information, a number of employees petitioned the Civil Service Commission to stop the agency reorganizations when they began. It was charged that these unrelated events were linked in a conspiracy. After four years of investigation, the commission concluded that, though there may have been some merit system violations in 1972, there was no evidence of such a conspiracy, nor any evidence that the reorganizations were politically inspired.[28]

News accounts of "investigations" and "merit violations" helped to cast further suspicion on the agency, causing congressional committees to warn the agency not to reorganize until all these controversies had been resolved:.

> In the meantime, however, the Committee cannot approve of the reorganizations you are planning. Recent media accounts suggest these plans may be a method "to remove 'troublemakers' supposedly protected by the Civil Service Regulations." While these allegations are being adjudicated or settled, the reorganizations should not be implemented.[29]

---

[27] See letter from Asa T. Briley, director, U.S. Civil Service Commission, San Francisco Region, to Charles W. Goady, regional director, ACTION, Region IX, February 27, 1974; letter from Robert E. Hampton, chairman, U.S. Civil Service Commission, to Senator Alan Cranston, chairman, Special Subcommittee on Human Resources, April 18, 1974.

[28] See U.S. Civil Service Commission, Bureau of Personnel Management Evaluation, "A Report on Alleged Political Influence and Other Improprieties in Personnel Matters at ACTION," mimeographed (Washington, D.C.: U.S. Civil Service Commission, November 18, 1975).

[29] Letter from Senator Warren G. Magnuson to ACTION Director Michael P. Balzano, January 15, 1975.

Since many of the allegations in the employee petition had been investigated for years, it was obvious that many more years might pass before the matter was fully aired. The resulting delay in the reorganization was precisely what the petitioners hoped to achieve.

Still others who petitioned the commission almost stopped the reorganization through intricate legal maneuvers. The chairman of a Senate subcommittee overseeing ACTION wrote:

> This proposal is made at a time when vacancies exist in both the position of Associate Director for Domestic and Anti-Poverty Operations (for over two months) and of the Associate Director for International Operations (for four months). Section 401 of P.L. 93-113 established these two positions statutorily (requiring Presidential nomination and Senate confirmation) in order to assure that there would be a single Agency official responsible for all aspects of domestic programs and one for all aspects of international programs. (The statutory language provides that each such Associate Director "shall carry out operations responsibility for all programs authorized under [, respectively,] This Act [P.L. 93-113], and . . . the Peace Corps Act. . . .") No nominations have been submitted to the Senate by the President for either of these positions and yet these major reorganizations are going forward with only an interim "Acting" head of DO and an interim "Acting" *deputy* head of the Office of International Operations.[30]

This proposition was ironic in that the committee staff had said no confirmation hearings would be held even if the President did submit nominations. This delay was in keeping with its earlier tactic of postponing the confirmation hearings for ACTION's deputy director for more than five months.[31]

After investigating the senator's complaint, the commission responded to the inquiry.

> There is, in our opinion, no basis for requiring ACTION to postpone the reorganization until all pending grievances and appeals arising from the downgrading actions have been resolved.
>
> The staff of our Bureau of Personnel Management Evaluation is working closely with officials of ACTION to assure that employee rights are protected. We note your concern that significant organizational changes are being made at a time when both the Associate Director for Domestic and Anti-

---

[30]December 30, 1974, letter from Senator Alan Cranston to Robert E. Hampton, p. 2.

[31]President Nixon nominated John L. Ganley to be the deputy director of ACTION on January 25, 1974. He was confirmed by the Senate on June 9, 1974.

Poverty Operations and Associate Director for International Operations positions are vacant. However, it is clearly not within the jurisidiction of the Civil Service Commission to challenge the authority of the Director of ACTION to restructure the organization of the agency, even though these two key positions are vacant.[32]

Philosophical Challenges. All attempts at integrating programs to achieve exchanges of ideas and services met with opposition, but changes in philosophical approaches to "social change" met with even greater opposition. The early days of the War on Poverty were characteristic of the times. The era of protest and demonstrations of the mid-1960s carried over into the poverty program. The politics of confrontation so dominated the VISTA program during the late 1960s that many of the program's earlier congressional supporters had turned against it. In 1973 we set out to change the national image of the agency from a program of confrontation with the establishment to one of working harmoniously with the establishment in a low-key fashion. The ACTION institutes sought to encourage the agency's staff to favor less volatile means for achieving social change. The staff was presented with goals drawn from the congressional hearings held when the programs were created.[33] These statements showed that the agency's goals had not changed.

The need for a low-key program was further demonstrated during the institutes by people who gave the staff their views of the programs. Agency personnel heard labor, ethnic, religious, and civic leaders tell of being excluded from participation in the programs because they were not racial minorities. Community leaders told of their initial willingness to work with antipoverty volunteers only to be treated as enemies of the people. Anonymous surveys of the staff before and after the institutes revealed that the employees were positively affected by the training. The majority of those who initially believed the agency's earlier course was correct came away believing that unless ACTION adopted more harmonious tactics it would not survive.[34]

The moment President Nixon announced ACTION's new goals in 1973, former ACTION staff members working in the Senate subcommittee overseeing our legislation challenged the legality of the new

---

[32]Letter from Robert E. Hampton, chairman, U.S. Civil Service Commission, to Senator Alan Cranston, February 4, 1975, p. 2.

[33]See Michael P. Balzano, *The Political and Social Ramifications of the VISTA Program: A Question of Ends and Means* (Ann Arbor, Mich.: University Microfilms, 1971), Ph.D. diss., Department of Government, Georgetown University, pp. 34–37, for a discussion of the congressional intent of VISTA's goals.

[34]University of Colorado, "ACTION Institutes," p. 285.

28

goals. In a series of meetings with agency staff and Senate aides, we were told that the goals were in conflict with the law, but after weeks of delay, no statute could be cited that rendered the goals illegal. The ACTION institutes, which had been so popular that many employees protested being excluded, were resurrected in a negative light. The commission was asked to investigate the institutes on the grounds that the agency had illegally attempted to change the philosophical beliefs of career civil servants. After more than two years of examining all of the charges, the commission ruled that changing the attitudes of employees with respect to changing social needs was proper.

> There can be no doubt that one purpose of the Institutes was to try to explain the agency's goals as Director Balzano saw them and to convince employees of the desirability of those goals. The above-quoted excerpts from the contract and affidavits make this quite clear.

> The question becomes, then, whether it is proper for an agency to attempt to influence its employees' thinking with respect to their official functions and responsibilities. We believe the answer is that such activity is clearly permissible. In fact, this is the obvious intent of many training courses (e.g., equal employment opportunity courses, supervisory training). Our only caveat is that it would not be proper for an agency to resort to "brainwashing" tactics, and we have seen no evidence that ACTION did so.[35]

The Civil Service Commission was also asked to investigate allegations that the agency's reorganizations and downgrades were politically inspired. It was alleged that the anonymous attitude surveys were secretly coded so that the respondents could be identified and rewarded or punished on the basis of their agreement or disagreement with the philosophical thrust of the ACTION goals. A lengthy, complex, and ultimately fruitless investigation was initiated by several congressional aides in an attempt to substantiate their theory of wrongdoing. Agency employees were summoned to Capitol Hill by congressional aides who cross-examined them for hours on this subject. In addition, the agency was deluged with congressional requests for information, which took hundreds of man hours to compile.[36] At senior staff meetings ACTION department heads complained that the manpower drain was seriously impairing their ability to operate the

---

[35] U.S. Civil Service Commission, "A Report on Alleged Political Influence at ACTION," p. 19.

[36] The following letters are examples of the labyrinthine depth to which this investigation was carried: letter from Senator Alan Cranston to ACTION Director Michael Balzano, November 7, 1974; letter from ACTION Director Michael Balzano to Senator Alan Cranston, December 5, 1974.

agency. ACTION's general counsel complained that the line between the congressional power of oversight and harassment had disappeared. After months of investigation and analysis of employee personnel records, the commission concluded that the allegations proved groundless.[37] A considerable portion of ACTION's problems in reorganizing and changing the program's philosophical thrust would not have occurred but for interference from congressional aides.[38]

The Threat of Dismantlement. The controversy reached a crescendo in early 1975 in what was billed as the first in a series of oversight hearings aimed at dismantling ACTION and returning its programs to the agencies from which they had come. Once again the controversy touched the White House. White House congressional liaison officers were informed by Senate staff members that unless the President removed the director, on grounds of mismanagement, Congress would dismantle the agency. Having already witnessed the antics of both the congressional and the agency staff, the White House turned a deaf ear to the whole subject.

The media gave the controversy intensive coverage, predicting total dismantling of the agency. The committee staff unofficially offered olive branches, suggesting that, if the reorganizations were ended, the hearings might never be scheduled. Nevertheless, the agency's management stood its ground and continued its reorganizations. The opening words of the presiding chairman of the hearings, before a standing-room-only crowd, described the congressional position as referee:

> We are primarily concerned with the programs, the philosophy underlying them, whether they can best operate in ACTION or in HEW or Community Services or some other agency.
>
> I would hope that the witnesses will try to really spend more time on this basic responsibility of the subcommittee and I think in that way we can conserve a lot of time if we try to confine ourselves to the underlying purposes of these programs and how they can best serve the people for whom they were constructed.

---

[37] Ibid., pp. 20–22.

[38] The following articles indicate the power congressional aides exercised over the agency: Charles Bartlett, "The Senate's High-Flying, Powerful Aides," *Washington Star*, May 26, 1975; Jeane Kirkpatrick, "New Bureaucracy Blooms on Hill," in "Letters to the Editor," *Washington Star*, July 1, 1975; Richard W. Murphy, "Are Lawmakers Losing Control?" in "Letters to the Editor," *Washington Star*, July 9, 1975; Charles Bartlett, "Voluntarism Vendettas in ACTION," *Chicago Sun–Times*, April 7, 1975; Inderjit Badhwar, "Balzano Weathers 'Vicious Attacks,'" *Federal Times*, vol. 11, no. 16 (June 25, 1975).

This is not personal but whether the Director, his subordinates or any employees of the Agency are good, bad or indifferent to the program, is not really the problem of this committee.

The same may be true of any other agency or administrative unit who administers the program. This committee, I can assure you, and I speak for all the members of the committee, has an open mind on the subject.[39]

Our opening remarks focused on the central issue:

Ours, Mr. Chairman, is a grass roots program. The communities, the poor people, the volunteers, the sponsors are throughout the country, not just in the Federal regional cities or the Washington headquarters.

In April 1973, when I took command of the ACTION Agency our total domestic personnel strength was 1,077. Mr. Chairman, if you had examined the distribution of ACTION employee resources in April of 1973, you would have found the following.

In headquarters, we had 778 people. In the domestic regional cities, we had 255 people and in the States we had 44 people covering some 800 programs.

Ours was a grass roots agency which existed at the tree-top level. The restructuring of our domestic regions, viewed in this light, clearly revealed the programmatic justification for it.[40]

In the end, the agency was given a clean bill of health by both the oversight committee and the Civil Service Commission.[41] The committee found no evidence of mismanagement of the agency and its programs, and the Civil Service Commission found no partisan motivation behind the reorganizations. In fact, it determined that personnel management at ACTION was fair and responsible, and that the reorganizations were needed to bring the programs into the 1970s. The cost, however, of the time-consuming investigations, lawsuits, and court hearings was tremendous, consuming thousands of man-hours over a four-year period. And the controversy so muddied the water that the real consequences of reorganizing a government agency were lost in the whirlpool of Washington debate.

---

[39]*Oversight Hearings on ACTION Agency,* pp. 173–174.

[40]Ibid., p. 196.

[41]Letter from Representative Augustus F. Hawkins and Representative John Buchanan to Representative John Brademas, May 6, 1975; letter from John D. R. Coles, director, Bureau of Personnel Management and Evaluation, U.S. Civil Service Commission, to ACTION Director Michael P. Balzano, February 4, 1976.

3
THE PRESIDENT'S REORGANIZATION PLAN

The Promises

Shortly before President Carter went to the Congress seeking the authority to reorganize the executive branch, he visited employees of several departments in an attempt to reassure civil servants that his reorganizations would have no adverse impact on their lives. In a manner of speaking, he sought to maintain his commitment to substantial change in the bureaucracy while protecting the bureaucrats from changes in their individual lives. In so doing, the President made three promises. The first was to work with the employees:

> I am not going to impose on you from above some instant change that might disrupt your life and make your effectiveness lessened. I want the ideas that come to me to originate with you.
> All of my Cabinet members, including Ray Marshall, understand that. So don't be fearful of change. The change will be initiated by you and will let you do a better job.
> We won't come up with any comprehensive reorganization plan for the Labor Department without you being intimately involved in the process. We are not going to try to get off in a corner somewhere and devise something and spring it on you.[1]

Second, he promised that not one federal employee would be demoted or dismissed because of a reorganization:

> You need not have any fear of the prospective changes that might be brought forward. No one will be discharged in the entire Federal Government as a result of reorganization. No

---

[1] Office of the White House Press Secretary, transcript of President Carter's remarks to employees of the Department of Labor, February 9, 1977, pp. 2 and 6.

one in the Federal Government will lose seniority or pay status.[2]

The President was so confident on this last point that he invited employees threatened with dismissal to appeal to him personally:

> I believe that it won't disrupt the lives of employees in government.
> So persons would come first, human beings would come first, and the change in the structure of government would not adversely affect your own professional careers under any circumstances. If it ever does, you contact me directly. I mean that. All my Cabinet officers have instructions to that effect.[3]

And, third, the President assured employees that normal attrition would be the chief device for absorbing the impact of any reorganizations:

> The reason I feel very easy about saying nobody will be fired or reduced in grade level or status because of reorganization is because I intend to do it through normal attrition. I don't know if you realize it or not, but on an average or in our Government we have about a 10 percent attrition rate per year. In other words, at the end of every year, we have had at least 10 percent of our people who have resigned or retired or who have been transferred because of their own intiative. And how to make flexible the assignment of personnel within that 10 percent is very easy. Over a four-year period of time, it is compounded, of course; that is, 40 percent of the people who change their status on their own initiative.[4]

By explaining the rationale behind his intention to reorganize the government and by reassuring the federal employees that such moves would not adversely affect them, the President hoped to build internal support for his plans.

As the President signed the bill granting him the power to reorganize the federal government, he reminded both the legislators and the press that reorganizing the federal bureaucracy was indeed a key issue in his bid for the presidency.

> I think of all the campaign speeches that I have made throughout the nation, the most consistent commitment that

---

[2] Office of the White House Press Secretary, transcript of President Carter's remarks to employees of the Department of the Treasury, February 10, 1977, p. 3.

[3] Office of the White House Press Secretary, transcript of President Carter's remarks to employees of the Department of Commerce, February 9, 1977, p. 16.

[4] Office of the White House Press Secretary, transcript of President Carter's remarks to employees of the Department of Health, Education, and Welfare, February 16, 1977, p. 6.

was made to the American people was that I would move as quickly as possible to improve the efficiency and the effectiveness and the sensitivity of the several government bureaucracies in dealing with the needs of the American people.

I believe it was one of the campaign issues that induced the American people to give me their support. . . .[5]

He also noted that he was entering an area filled with problems: "It is going to be a long and very challenging undertaking. There are going to be a lot of controversies, but I am determined to do a good job with it."[6]

The Problems

Although President Carter will unquestionably exercise greater power, prestige, and influence than ACTION could, he will probably encounter most of the roadblocks that we did. Given the goals the President seeks to reach and his self-imposed restrictions against demoting or dismissing a single employee, some problems can be easily predicted.

Every indication is that the President will attempt to streamline the government through mergers and consolidations. ACTION is an agency born out of such an attempt. We know from experience that any benefits from a merger must come from the consolidation of transferred administrative systems. For the President to use consolidations successfully, he must deal with at least three variables: the Congress, his own presidential appointees, and the federal employees in the agencies involved.

In order to streamline government bureaucracy by eliminating duplication, either the duplicating programs must be consolidated or some of the programs must be discontinued while others are strengthened. In either case, the changes will arouse congressmen whose spheres of influence are affected. Those who sit on congressional committees having oversight on particular programs will not want to lose jurisdiction over those areas. Reorganization would negate their years of experience and expertise, their reputations as authorities in a certain area, and their control over matters vital to their constituency. Joseph A. Califano, who was appointed secretary of HEW by President Carter, vividly describes this congressional obstacle:

---

[5] Office of the White House Press Secretary, transcript of President Carter's remarks upon signing the Reorganization Act of 1977, April 6, 1977.

[6] Ibid.

Reorganizations are enormously difficult to achieve politically. In the Congress, committee members covet their jurisdictions as bees protect their hives; taking away any honey without being stung is not a task for political amateurs. They have potent allies among their parochial cohorts in the legislative branch, the executive bureaucracy, and the special interests that are aroused by any attempt to disturb existing cozy relationships.

The investment of political capital is so great and the risk of loss so substantial that a president can at best achieve one or two major reorganizations during his years in office—if he selects his targets shrewdly.[7]

It would be incorrect to assume that presidential appointees will blindly follow orders, especially when such orders might reduce the scope of an agency or department. Again, the President should profit from the experience of Mr. Califano, who became a seasoned veteran in the mechanics of government reorganization during the Johnson administration.

And the president needs some help from his own cabinet and agency heads, which is rarely forthcoming. With one exception (John Gardner), in the scores of reorganization proposals I considered while on the White House staff, the cabinet officer or agency destined to lose a program in a reorganization opposed the plan.[8]

On numerous occasions, the power struggle between ACTION department heads, including presidential appointees, slowed scheduled transfers of functions for months. At the root of the delays, we usually found an effort either to preserve the status quo in a program or to maintain the personnel or budget under the control of a particular department.

In 1975 the President asked us to prepare a bare bones budget for congressional approval, one that did not weaken the programs but kept expenses to a minimum. After we prepared such a budget, we discovered that a presidentially appointed associate director went to Congress and successfully lobbied for the addition of $14 million beyond the budget the President had approved. Such lobbying was in direct violation of the instructions of both the President and OMB. Ironically, this money could not be spent in existing budget categories.

Mergers and consolidations will without question disturb the status quo of the departments or agencies affected, and federal em-

[7] Joseph A. Califano, Jr., *A Presidential Nation* (New York: W. W. Norton and Company, Inc., 1975), p. 27.
[8] Ibid., p. 25.

ployees will adopt a protectionist view of "their" program. Any merger will diminish the public visibility of at least some of the affected programs and can be expected to meet with resistance, even if the merger is a simple paper transfer of one agency to another. When the ACTION merger took place, the Peace Corps director became the director of ACTION, and not one Peace Corps employee was reduced in rank, grade, or salary. Yet, many employees and congressmen still bemoan the transfer, in the belief that it had a detrimental effect on the program by reducing public visibility for the Peace Corps.

Mergers and consolidations imply the possibility of changes in grades, salaries, and duty stations. Understandably, this possibility gives rise to fears and opposition, which could become the President's greatest obstacle. As the President begins to consolidate the scores of agencies and departments, thousands of employees in hundreds of areas will be affected by the mergers. If two or more agencies are merged, the resulting superagency would not need two or more offices of the general counsel, of equal employment opportunity, of administration and finance, of public affairs, of congressional liaison, et cetera.[9] The new superagency would obviously take advantage of economies of scale by eliminating duplication, but where would the employees who had performed the eliminated services be relocated? Having been promised they would not suffer loss of grade, pay or job, would they all be allowed to stay with their present salary and status?

Threats to employee livelihood will be perceived not only in the transfer of programs from one department to another but also in shifts in authority from one part of an agency to another. Both President Carter and OMB Director Bert Lance have said a shift in decision-making approval to lower levels of the bureaucracy is a goal of reorganization. In a major department like HEW, thousands of employees could be affected. This shift of authority will result in changes in job descriptions and downgrades. Hence, under present Civil Service regulations, the President's promise not to reduce anyone's rank or salary cannot be kept. The only way to avoid such downgrades would be either to abandon the idea of local control or to continue paying the affected employees the same salary, regardless of their diminished responsibility. One alternative would run contrary to the President's promise to make government more responsive to the needs of the

[9] This economy of scale was precisely what the ACTION merger was designed to accomplish. All of these support services would have to be re-created, for example, to restore the Peace Corps to its former independent status, and would result in an additional cost to the federal government of about $10 million annually. See memorandum from Emerson Markham, director, Budget Division, ACTION, to Elizabeth Prestridge, executive assistant to the director, ACTION, January 3, 1977, for an explanation of these costs.

people, and the other would violate Civil Service rules.

Veteran journalists who cover the federal beat have already questioned whether the President's promises can be kept. The promises, it has been said, imply that an omelette can be made without breaking a single egg.

The Federal Work Force

Americans, especially those operating businesses, are mindful of the general presence of big government, but few are aware of the full dimensions of its cost. Excluding the military, the federal payroll comprises 2,556,753 full-time employees. By most standards, they are well compensated indeed. The average federal employee in Washington, D.C., earns $17,541 per year, in addition to a generous package of benefits.[10] Federal employees join a retirement system that is far superior to the social security system covering most Americans. A federal employee earning $25,000 annually can retire at age fifty-five, after thirty years of service, and receive $14,640 per year, or 56 percent of base pay.[11]

One indication of the relative comfort of the federal work force emerged from a poll taken in a Washington suburban area.[12] The poll showed that residents of the suburban Washington area are less concerned about inflation than is the general population. Government workers receive almost automatic cost-of-living increases each year and are, therefore, comparatively unharmed by inflation.

According to recent Gallup poll data, 64 percent of the national sample believed that federal workers are paid more for equivalent work than employees in the private sector.[13] And thousands of federal employees are paid at levels beyond that allowed by the law, because, according to personnel classification desk audits, a great proportion of the federal work force is overgraded. In an audit of 1,800 positions at HEW, 550 were found to be overgraded.[14] By how much these positions are overgraded is unclear. At ACTION, the Civil Service

[10]U.S. Civil Service Commission, Bureau of Manpower Information Systems, *Pay Structure of the Federal Civil Service,* SM 33–76.

[11]U.S. Civil Service Commission, Bureau of Retirement, Insurance and Occupational Health, "Certificate of Membership in the United States Civil Service Retirement System," FPM Suppl. 831–1, September 1975.

[12]"To Live in the Land of Milk and Honey . . . Go to the Suburbs of Washington," *Sindlinger's Economic Service,* issue 1141–42, p. 2910.

[13]George Gallup, "Federal Workers Held in Low Public Esteem," *Washington Post,* June 12, 1977.

[14]Letter from David Matthews, secretary of Health, Education, and Welfare, to James T. Lynn, director, Office of Management and Budget, September 3, 1976.

Commission found misclassifications as great as *five grades*: a position that should have been a GS-9, earning $14,100, was held by a GS-14, earning $28,725.

Despite the antibureaucracy sentiment that helped propel the President into office, and despite the recent polls demonstrating the public's continued demand for cost efficiencies, there are forces moving in the opposite direction. At the present time, several bills have been introduced in the House of Representatives to protect federal employees from being reduced in pay or rank for as long as they remain in the position they occupy, even if the agency has determined that they are overpaid for that position. Congressman Robert N. C. Nix (Democrat, Pennsylvania), the sponsor of one such bill, said:

> Demotions caused by downgrading of positions are one of the most pressing problems of the Government's civil service workforce. Thousands of positions may be downgraded shortly which will have the devastating effect of demoralizing the dedicated employees involved as well as severely hampering their career advancement. It is incumbent on the Congress to act with dispatch on this issue and, therefore, I have introduced a bill which will correct the inequities inherent in this process.
>
> For the most part, the downgrading of a position is through no fault of the employee. Yet the major impact of such determinations is felt almost exclusively by the employee.
>
> This bill will protect these employees by providing that they would retain their grade and salary for as long as they hold that position.[15]

If the public is made aware of this legislation and fully understands its ramifications, this bill is likely to cause considerable controversy. It is difficult to imagine that the average taxpayer, who earns $11,000 a year, will support tens of thousands of federal workers unjustifiably earning an average of $15,000 a year until retirement.

The Possibilities of Employee Attrition

The President correctly reasons that employee attrition will enable him to reduce the total work force while avoiding the hardship of demotion or dismissal for nonretiring employees. ACTION also relied on attrition to reduce its ranks and to avoid terminating employees. But this tool had severe limitations. If all hiring were frozen, even temporarily, all areas of the agency would be subject to personnel shortages. A

---

[15] U.S. Congress, House of Representatives, *Congressional Record*, April 26, 1977, E2475.

vacancy might occur in a critical area, such as the office of the budget or general counsel or the personnel office, and to leave the position unfilled could eliminate a vitally needed function. Moreover, a policy of attrition assumes equality among all those who depart from the work force. If a key manager retired or died, would this position go unfilled? If the only secretary in an office left, would no one assume this workload?

ACTION learned that to use attrition properly the agency had to have a carefully worked out plan, including a sagacious use of temporary employees. A temporary employee earns the same salary as the regular employee minus the benefits. As vacancies occurred, temporary employees were hired to perform a function while it was being phased out or decentralized. When that happened, the temporary was either relocated to a similar task or separated.

The overall plan indicated which positions could be allowed to remain unfilled, thus taking advantage of attrition. Although ACTION was a small agency, with relatively few programs and relatively uncomplicated functions, each plan had to be carefully tailored to a central agency function, such as recruiting, programming, or training. Each small plan was constantly monitored against the agency's total objectives. Our plans dealt with offices and divisions with fewer than 100 employees, and ACTION's entire domestic force consisted of fewer than 1,200 employees. For the President to accomplish his objectives through attrition, a detailed plan would have to be produced for each government agency in conjunction with a master plan, which pictured simultaneous movements throughout the entire federal government.

By using temporaries to fill vacancies resulting from attrition, ACTION was extremely successful in keeping forced terminations to a minimum. Many ACTION employees were able to transfer to other government agencies because it was a period of relative government stability: while ACTION was reorganizing, other agencies and departments throughout the federal government were free to hire. If the President tries to streamline the entire federal government, there will be very few places to which such employees can transfer.

The Federal Employee Unions

One of the ironies of the 1976 presidential election was that Jimmy Carter, the so-called anti-Washington candidate, received the solid support of the federal work force—employee unions and all. The candidate who pledged to clean up "the mess"—big government, the massive bureaucracy, the regulatory agencies—received such support from the bureaucracy that on the morning of November 3 a sign was placed in the lobby at ACTION which read, "We won!"

Why would federal employees applaud the victory of a President pledged to reducing their authority, income, and numbers? A reorganization of only two agencies could adversely affect thousands of employees. What will the President do with the surplus employees from an eliminated function? Will they stay on with no duties, and with no reduction in pay? What will happen to employees ordered to move elsewhere because of reorganization who will not go? Can we assume that Congress and the American people will allow tens of thousands of such employees, with salaries averaging over $15,000 per year, to remain in this status until they retire? The federal employee unions will certainly fight to retain every employee at full pay. Undoubtedly, they will take their fight to Congress, and 2.5 million federal employees will have the ear of Congress. Their power was well demonstrated when they influenced Congress to override President Ford's veto of the 7 percent pay raise in 1975.

Suppose the President concludes that the price of reorganizing the government is to retain all affected employees at full pay until they retire. The unions would lobby Congress to support that decision. What would happen if a congressman found himself between the pressures of a powerful union force and a tide of irate taxpayers, who, when they compared their own annual incomes with those of federal employees, demanded congressional opposition to this provision? The President might be willing to risk outraging the American taxpayer, on the assumption that the people would forget by the presidential election, but a congressman, facing these same voters more frequently, might be reluctant to take that risk. On the other hand, in view of the costs of retaining thousands of unneeded employees until retirement, the President may well reassess his earlier promises not to demote or dismiss a single federal employee.

There is indeed a precedent for such a drastic reversal in positions. On April 2, 1977, in his first nationally televised fireside chat, the President astounded Washington civil servants when he announced a presidential policy in keeping with his campaign promise to bring the Washington bureaucracy under control: "I will also request the Cabinet members to read all regulations personally before they are released."[16] Within three weeks, the President's cabinet persuaded the President of the physical impossibility of keeping such a promise. It is conceivable that, given the need to reduce the size and cost of government, the President will have to abandon promises made to the federal employees as well.

[16] Text of President Carter's televised address, *New York Times*, April 3, 1977, pp. 22–23.

4
CONCLUSION

The President was correct when he said that in reorganizing the federal government there will be "a lot of controversies." But, whatever obstacles he must overcome will be worthwhile if he is successful in reducing the size and cost of the bureaucracy while increasing its efficiency.

A massive series of consolidations could easily reduce the number of government agencies on paper without reducing the size, cost, and authority of the federal work force. In the 1980 presidential election, however, no one will be impressed with government flow charts that show a smaller government in theory but not in fact. Merely cosmetic attempts to streamline the government would scarcely escape exposure. Already the columnists who cover the federal government maintain a constant vigil on the statistics concerning the federal employees. It has already been noted, for example, that since President Carter issued a government-wide freeze on new hires in order to maximize the impact of attrition, the decrease in federal employees has been minuscule.

In 1980, political scientists, students of public administration, and presidential aspirants can ask a number of questions that have quantifiable answers that are easily ascertained: Has the number of federal employees decreased, increased, or has it remained the same as in 1976? Is the volume of federal regulations larger or smaller than it was in 1976? And do the American people feel any less harassed by their government? The President's reelection may well depend on how he answers these questions.

Cover and book design: Pat Taylor